The Divine Council, Powers, and Principalities

A Brief Explanation of Territorial Spirits.

Rev. James Rudd
www.reverencejournal.com

The Divine Council, Powers, and Principalities
Copyright © 2022 Rev. James Rudd
All rights reserved.

www.reverencejournal.com

TABLE OF CONTENTS

Chapter 1:
Why This Matters (Pt. 1)   6

Chapter 2:
The Old Testament Concept of the Divine Council   11
    Other Mesopotamian Views of a Divine Council/Assembly   15
    The Terms "Elohim" and "Yahweh"   16
    Is the Hebrew Divine Council Monotheistic, Henotheistic, or Polytheistic?   20
    The Divine Council and the Tower of Babel   22
    The Captivity and Second Temple Period   28

Chapter 3:
The New Testament Concept of Powers and Principalities   34
    Powers and Principalities in 1 Pe, Rom, and 1 Cor   38
    Powers and Principalities in Ephesians   41
    Powers and Principalities in Colossians   44

Chapter 4:
Why This Matters (Pt. 2)   49

BIBLIOGRAPHY   52

4

Chapter 1:
Why This Matters (Pt. 1)

According to a 2019 Pew Research poll, the number of Americans identifying as atheists has doubled since 2009. Sounds alarming right? Maybe, maybe not. In 2009, only 2% of Americans identified as atheists. In 2019 that number had doubled, to 4%. An additional 5% of Americans identify themselves as agnostic.[1] The increase in Americans identifying as atheists or agnostics has spawned a fresh wave of apologetic seminars and books equipping believers to defend belief in a god from the growing atheist and agnostic population.

To put this increase in atheism and agnosticism into perspective, for every atheist/agnostic, there are nine Americans that believe in some sort of god or higher power. America is overwhelmingly theistic and overwhelmingly diverse in it's religious practices. This dynamic is called "Religious Pluralism"[2] and results in a sort of polytheistic[3] society. As a Pastor of nearly 20 years, polytheism (the belief in many gods), rather than atheism (the belief in no gods), appears to be the bigger challenge facing the church in America.

---

[1] https://www.pewresearch.org/fact-tank/2019/12/06/10-facts-about-atheists/

[2] Religious pluralism is the idea that multiple religions are permitted to coexist within a society.

[3] Polytheism is the belief in many or multiple gods.

While I certainly support the emphasis on defending the faith against a rise in atheism, I am also keenly aware of the much greater need to help Christians learn how to navigate a society that believes in many gods. Christians need to know what the Bible says about the existence of multiple spiritual beings, how this came to be and how we relate to this reality as followers of Jesus.

Atheism was hardly one of the most significant issues facing the authors of the Old and New Testaments of the Christian Bible. Rarely do the Biblical writers wrestle with the question of whether spiritual beings exist—it is presumed that they do. The Hebrew Old Testament and the Greek New Testament both emerged out of polytheistic contexts, and the surrounding peoples would have almost certainly had some sort of supernatural worldview that recognized the existence of spiritual beings. As theologian and missiologist Clinton Arnold writes; "The nations around Israel worshiped a multiplicity of gods and goddesses. In every century and every geographical region, including Palestine, the Jews lived in a polytheistic environment."[4] Assuming that this is the case, the Bible should be perfectly suited to equip the church to navigate a religiously pluralistic society, since the Bible itself emerged from just such a context.

---

[4] Clinton E. Arnold. *Powers of Darkness: Principalities and Powers in Paul's Letters*. (Downers Grove, IL: IVP Academic, 1992), 56.

The prerogative of the biblical writers was not so much to convince their readers that a spiritual realm existed, but rather to explain to their readers how the spiritual realm (1) came into being, (2) was populated, (3) functioned, and (4) was organized. Questions like "How did all of these spiritual beings come to exist?" and "Which spiritual being is more powerful?" or "What are the attributes of the spiritual beings?" or "What spiritual beings are present in some places as opposed to others?" or "Why do different people in different places worship different gods?" were the types of topics that the biblical writers were trying to address and are also the types of questions that this work will seek to address.

Overwhelmingly, the Biblical writers were comparing and contrasting various forms of polytheism with Hebrew and Christian monotheism. For example, in the Old Testament, this contrast took the form of conflicts between Yahweh and the gods of Egypt (see the plagues in Exod 7-11) or as contrasts between Yahweh and the Canaanite god Molech (Gen 22) or the Philistine god Dagon (1 Sam 5). Similarly, in the New Testament, there is a conflict between Jesus and various spiritual powers, principalities, rulers, and authorities that were recognized by the Jewish audience. This conflict is ultimately resolved at the cross and subsequently explained in the New Testament epistles.

A biblical framework for a spiritual realm is developed throughout the pages of the Bible. This biblical perspective establishes who the authoritative spiritual being is, what He is like, what differentiates Him from other spiritual beings, how He conducts His rule over the world, whether other spiritual beings exist and how these other spiritual beings came into existence and relate to one another. As we will see, *The Old Testament concept of the Divine Council will become the foundation for the New Testament concept of powers, principalities, rulers, and authorities.*

Chapter 2:
The Old Testament Concept of the Divine Council

The Hebrew people of the Old Testament had a supernatural or spiritual worldview. Not only did they believe in a supreme creator-deity named "Yahweh", but they also believed in an entire category of spiritual beings called "*elohim*". This concept, structure or system is often referred to as the "Divine Council". Essentially, the Divine Council refers to all the other spiritual beings that Yahweh interacts with as He rules the world that He alone created.

As E.T. Mullen points out, the term "Divine Council" is essentially synonymous with other Old Testament terms like "Divine Assembly", "Council of the Gods", "Heavenly Host" and "Sons of God" [5]. Any of these terms refer to "A group of heavenly beings other than Yahweh...."[6] Yahweh was the supreme and sole creator-deity who oversaw the Divine Council. Among the members of the Divine Council, Yahweh alone had attributes like omnipresence, omniscience and

---

[5] E. T. Mullen, Jr. "Divine Assembly" in *The Anchor Yale Bible Dictionary* edited by David Noel Freedman. (New York: Doubleday, 1992), 9.

[6] Karl Van Der Toorn, Bob Becking and Pieter W. Van Der Horst, eds. *Dictionary of Deities and Demons in the Bible*. (Leiden, The Netherlands: Brill Publishing, 1999), 794.

omnipotence. For the purposes of this work the term "Divine Council," as used in Ps 82:1 (ESV), will be used to refer to this concept.

Samuel A. Meier describes the Divine Council: "God's council was composed of numerous supernatural creatures associated with the stars and planets and the rule of the cosmos: 'all the host of heaven' (1 Ki 22:19), the 'sons of God' (Job 1:6, 2:1), and 'seraphs were in attendance above him' (Isa 6:2)."[7] Meir continues; "The divine council is the body to whom God characteristically reveals His plans...."[8] Prior to the exile prophets had privileged access to the council (Amos 3:7), access that seems to diminish as Israel is increasingly unfaithful.

Perhaps no passages better establish the Hebrew perspective of the Divine Council than Psalms 82 and 89. Foremost expert on the Divine Council, Michael Heiser suggests: "Psalm 82 is an essential text for understanding the Israelite Divine Council. The psalm contains an explicit reference to a Divine Assembly under the authority of God (*elohim*) along with a subsequent plural use of the word *elohim* ('God, gods')."[9] Psalm 82:1-2, 6-7 (ESV) states:

---

[7] Samuel A. Meier. *Themes and Transformations in Old Testament Prophecy*. (Downers Grove, IL: IVP Academic, 2009), 21.
[8] Meier, *Themes and Transformations*, 24.
[9] Michael S. Heiser. "Divine Council" in *Dictionary of Old Testament: Prophets* edited by Mark J.

> God has taken His place in the divine council;
> in the midst of the gods [*elohim*] He holds judgment:
> How long will you judge unjustly and show partiality to the wicked?
>
> I said 'You are gods [*elohim*], sons of the Most High, all of you;
> nevertheless, like men you shall die,
> and fall like any prince.

In Psalm 82 Yahweh is essentially berating Divine Council members (other, lesser spiritual beings) for not ruling according to His character. He promises judgment on these spiritual beings. Likewise, in Psalm 89:5-8 (Legacy Standard Bible, hereafter LSB) the psalmist writes:

> The heavens will praise Your wonders, O Yahweh;
> Your faithfulness also in the assembly of the holy ones.
> For who in the sky is comparable to Yahweh?
> Who among the sons of the mighty is like Yahweh,
> A God greatly dreaded in the council of the holy ones,

Boda and J. Gordon McConville, 162-166. (Downers Grove, IL: IVP Academic, 2012), 162-163.

> And fearsome above all those who are around Him?
> O Yahweh God of hosts, who is like You, O mighty Yah?

Here, the psalmist reflects on the unique place that Yahweh holds among the other spiritual beings. None among the council are comparable or as mighty. The other council members dread Yahweh. The stanza ends with the rhetorical question; "who is like You, O mighty Yah?" The implied answer is "No one is like Yahweh." This belief in the unique and incomparable nature of Yahweh is foundational to Hebrew and Christian monotheism.

While it is unclear exactly when these other spiritual beings came into existence, Job 38:4-7 indicates that by the time of the creation of the earth the council members were already in existence; "Where were you when I laid the foundations of the earth?... When the morning stars sang together and all the sons of God shouted for joy?" In this passage, the phrase; "morning stars" is a reference to spiritual beings (that's why they can sing). Obviously, these spiritual beings existed after Yahweh, but before the earth was created.

Other Mesopotamian Views of a Divine Council/Assembly

The Hebrews were not the only people who held this type of supernatural worldview, consisting of multiple spiritual beings. Canaanites, Egyptians, Phoenicians and especially the people of Ugarit all held similar views. According to Heiser, "All ancient Mediterranean cultures had some conception of a divine council." [10] Of all the foreign perspectives on the divine council, perhaps the one that most closely resembles the view of the Hebrews was the Ugarit Assembly of El. As Heiser writes,

> The council at Ugarit apparently had four tiers (Smith 2001, 41–53). The top tier consisted of El and his wife Athirat (Asherah). The second tier was the domain of their royal family ("sons of El"; "princes"). One member of this second tier served as the vicegerent of El and was, despite being under El's authority, given the title "most high" (Wyatt, 419). A third tier was for "craftsman deities," while the lowest tier was reserved for the messengers (ml'km), essentially

---

[10] Michael S. Heiser. "Divine Council" in *Dictionary of the Old Testament: Wisdom, Poetry and Writings* edited by Peter Enns and Tremper Longman III, 112-116. (Downers Grove, IL: IVP Academic, 2008), 112.

servants or staff.[11]

The idea that the spiritual beings inhabiting the spiritual realm were tiered is helpful in understanding the Hebrew divine council. A tiered system indicates that distinctions exist. Some spiritual beings rank higher than other spiritual beings. Much of the structure of the Hebrew divine council can be established by defining two key terms, "*elohim*" and "Yahweh."

The Terms "Elohim" and "Yahweh"

The Hebrew word אֱלֹהִים (*elohim*) is translated "rulers, judges...divine ones... angels ... gods"[12] The term is applied to a wide variety of beings in the Hebrew Bible; "*ĕlōhîm*; most commonly refers to God (e.g., Gen 1:1) but can also refer to angels (8:5; cf. Job 1:6; 2:1), pagan deities (Pss 96:4,5; 97:7,9; 135:5), or even humans such as the king (45:6), judges (Exod 21:6; 22:8–9), or a leader like Moses (Exod 4:16; 7:1)."[13] Heiser expands the concept further; "the word refers to any inhabitant of the unseen spiritual world. That's why you'll find it used of God Himself (Gen 1:1), demons

---

[11] Heiser, *Wisdom, Poetry and Writings*, 115.
[12] Francis Brown, S.R. Driver and Charles A. Briggs, *The Brown-Driver-Briggs Hebrew and English Lexicon.* (Peabody, MA: Hendrickson Publications, 1996), 43.
[13] D. A. Carson. *NIV Biblical Theology Study Bible,* (Grand Rapids, MI: Zondervan, 2018), Study Notes on Psalm 82.

(Deut 32:17) and the human dead in the afterlife (1 Sam 28:13)." [14]

In his book "*The Unseen Realm*," Michael Heiser further illustrates the use of "*elohim*":

> The biblical writers refer to a half-dozen different entities with the word *elohim*. By any religious accounting, the attributes of those entities are *not* equal.
> - Yahweh, the God of Israel (thousands of times - eg., Gen 2:4-5; Deut 4:35)
> - The members of Yahweh's council (Ps 82:1, 6)
> - Gods and goddesses of other nations (Judg 11:24; 1 Kgs 11:33)
> - Demons (Hebrew: *shedim* - Deut 32:17)
> - The deceased Samuel (1 Sam 28:13)
> - Angels or the Angel of Yahweh (Gen 35:7) [15]

Noticeably absent from the lists above are animals, plants, and other natural/material creatures. Inanimate objects are also not considered *elohim*.

Even with all of the various applications of the term, it is clear that *elohim* is not a personal name for the Hebrew God, but more like a categorical term that can be applied to many types of spiritual beings. In fact,

---

[14] Heiser, Michael S, *Supernatural: What the Bible Teaches about the unseen world - and why it matters.* (Bellingham, WA: Lexham Press, 2015), 20.

[15] Heiser, *Supernatural*, 30.

translating the term *elohim* as "gods" may contribute to some of the confusion surrounding the term, since many modern readers ascribe a certain set of attributes (i.e. omniscience, omnipotence, omnipresence, eternality, etc…) to the term "god" that is not necessarily reflected by each being referred to as an *elohim* in the Old Testament. It is possible that using the phrase "spiritual beings" might be a more effective translation of *elohim* for a modern audience. This is the approach of the Bible Project in their videos addressing this topic.[16] For the purpose of this work, the phrase "spiritual beings" will be used when referring to *elohim*.

In contrast to the categorical term "*elohim*" is the personal name "Yahweh." "Yahweh," often translated "Jehovah" or "The LORD" is the proper, personal name of the Hebrew God and is understood to mean "the existing One."[17] The name Yahweh only refers to one being in the entire Hebrew Bible, the God of Israel. This is the name that is revealed to Moses in Exod 3. The implication of Yahweh meaning "the existing One" is that Israel has no theogony—no origin story for their God—since Yahweh is eternal. The absence of any theogony (origin story) would have caused Israel to stand out among other nations. While the other nations

---

[16] https://youtu.be/U5iyUik97Lg
[17] Francis Brown, S.R. Driver and Charles A. Briggs, *The Brown-Driver-Briggs Hebrew and English Lexicon*. (Peabody, MA: Hendrickson Publications, 1996).

had a story to explain the existence of their god, Israel's God didn't have a story of coming into existence—He just always had existed. This made Yahweh unique, or, in other words, holy.

To compare and contrast the two terms, Yahweh is an *elohim*, but not all *elohim* are Yahweh. Yahweh is the supreme *elohim*—the self-existing creator of all the other *elohim*—the only one whose existence is independent of all others. By way of illustration, one could say that "Adam is a man, but not all men are Adam." "Man" is a category, like *elohim*. "Adam" is a personal name, like Yahweh.

When Psalm 82:6 refers to the Divine Council it uses the term "*elohim*" but not "Yahweh." God's "staff team" or "task force" are all referred to as *elohim,* (it's a plural noun in Hebrew). Later, in Psalm 89:5, the Divine Council is referred to as "the assembly of the holy ones." This assembly or council is gathered to Yahweh (translated "LORD"). The *elohim* gather around Yahweh, who is, Himself, the supreme, self-existing *elohim*. Many literal translations like the NASB, the ESV and the LSB mark this distinction by capitalizing "God" when it refers to Yahweh but leaving it lowercase and plural ("gods") when referring to other spiritual beings.

Is the Hebrew Divine Council Monotheistic, Henotheistic, or Polytheistic?

In the Hebrew Bible there are many spiritual beings or divine ones, but only one supreme deity, Yahweh. The supreme Hebrew Deity's name means; "the existing One" because He has no beginning. The Hebrew people had no theogony, which made their worldview unique. The eternal presence of the supreme deity is one of the distinctives of the Hebrew religion, resulting in a monotheistic worldview, distinct from the polytheism of both the Old and New Testament contexts.

A perceptive person may ask; "How is the Hebrew Divine Council not polytheistic or henotheistic?" While polytheism is "the belief in a multitude of distinct and separate deities…,"[18] henotheism is the belief that there are many gods, but that one's own personal god should be favored or prioritized among the many gods. Henotheism is contrary to monotheism in that it does not clearly or adequately distinguish between lesser spiritual beings that are without certain non-communicable attributes and thus are unworthy of worship, while Yahweh alone possesses those non-communicable attributes and is the only one worthy to be favored and worshiped.

---

[18] Walter A. Elwell, ed, *Evangelical Dictionary of Theology, 2nd Ed.* (Grand Rapids, MI: Baker Academic, 2006), 931.

While the Hebrew Divine Council does recognize the existence of many spiritual beings, it does not recognize all spiritual beings as equal. As previously stated, among the *elohim* are Yahweh, angelic messengers, demons, disembodied humans, and more. Yet, among the category of *elohim* there is only one spiritual being who is eternal, creator, all-present, all-knowing, all-powerful, worthy of worship and whose existence is independent of all others—Yahweh. As Mullen points out, "...members of [the] council are presumed to be clearly inferior to Yahweh."[19] Micheal Heiser explains the distinction between Yahweh and the rest of the *elohim*:

> Polytheism and monolatrous henotheism both presume 'species sameness' among the gods...Although Yahweh was an *elohim*, he was qualitatively unique among the *elohim*. The primary distinguishing characteristic of Yahweh from any other *elohim* was his preexistence and creation of all things...Yahweh's utter uniqueness against all other *elohim* is monotheism on ancient semitic terms, and orthodox Israelite religion reflects this at all stages.[20]

---

[19] Mullen, *Divine Council*, 10.
[20] Heiser, *Wisdom, Poetry and Writings,* 114.

The Hebrew Bible itself communicates this concept in Psalm 97:9; "For You are Yahweh Most High over all the earth; You are exalted far above all gods [*elohim*]."

The Divine Council and the Tower of Babel

One of the most significant stories relating to the development of the Hebrew Divine Council is the story of the Tower of Babel in Gen 11. The events of Babel immediately pick up after the story of Noah and the flood and are critical to the understanding of how the Hebrew concept of the Divine Council is foundational to the New Testament concept of powers and principalities.

A significant amount of time has passed between the stories of the flood and the Tower of Babel, as the earth has been repopulated to some degree. A table of seventy nations (families) that have descended from Noah and his three sons is identified in Gen 10. At the point of the story of Babel the entire human race is speaking the same language, has developed some type of brick-making technology, and is beginning to have ambitions for greatness (Gen 11:1-4). Later in the Old Testament Babel evolves into Babylon, which carries significant metaphorical meaning throughout both the Old and New Testaments and helps to provide a narrative arch for the redemptive story.

Under the rule of Nimrod (Gen 10:10 - whose name can mean "valiant" or "rebel"), the people of Babel determined to build a city for the stated purpose of not being scattered "over the face of the earth" (Gen 11:4 LSB). It is also possible that this tower is built as a guard against another flood. If this is the case this would serve as another instance of the human race not taking Yahweh at His word, as He had previously made a covenant not to flood the earth again (Gen 9:11).

The plan to centralize in Babel appears to be contrary to Yahweh's desire for humanity to fill, subdue and rule the earth (Gen 1:28). As a result, the plan backfires when Yahweh observes their work and states; "Come, let Us go down and there confuse their language, so that they will not understand one another's language." (Gen 11:7 LSB) It is generally agreed upon by scholars that the plural pronoun "Us" used in this passage is a reference to Yahweh's court, assembly or council. The NIV Biblical Theology Study Bible suggests that: "The plural pronoun may reflect the divine court...[21]" Bible scholars Michael Heiser[22] and John Walton[23] share this conviction.

As a result of the confused language, the people are scattered throughout the earth, each language group

---

[21] Carson, *Biblical Theology,* Note on Gen 11:7.
[22] Heiser, *Unseen Realm*, 350.
[23] John H. Walton, *Ancient Near Eastern Thought and the Old Testament 2nd Ed.* (Grand Rapids, MI: Baker Academic, 2018), 56.

going its own separate way, presumably. Yet, it is in Moses' recollection of the Babel story, found in Deut 32, that the spiritual reality of the scattering at Babel is further developed. Heiser identifies the connection between Gen 11 and the Song of Moses: "Deuteronomy 32.8-9 describes how Yahweh's dispersal of the nations at Babel resulted in His disinheriting those nations as His people..."[24]

Heiser also clearly communicates the ramifications of such an interpretation: "In Dt. 32.8-9...when the nations were divided at the Tower of Babel incident, the nations were placed by God under the authority of lesser *elohim* [spiritual beings]...."[25] Essentially, Heiser and others are suggesting that when the people scattered at Babel, the confusing spirits scattered among them and that the people were given over to these confusing spirits. This was an act of judgment by Yahweh. A pattern emerges in Gen 3-11 whereby human beings reject the leadership of Yahweh in favor of lesser *elohim* (i.e. the serpent in the garden). As humans reject Yahweh's leadership in favor of lesser *elohim*, Yahweh hands the rebellious people over to the consequence of their sin as a form of judgment.

The way in which Deut 32:8 is interpreted does depend on the translation in use. For instance, the NASB and LSB both say that the "boundaries of the

---

[24] Heiser, *Unseen Realm,* 113.
[25] Ibid, 34.

people" are "according to the sons of Israel." This reading seems anachronistic as at the time of the Tower of Babel Israel was neither a person, a place nor a people. The ESV conveys that the "borders of the peoples" are "according to the number of the sons of God" (with "sons of God" being synonymous with the Divine Council) and the NRSV says that the "boundaries of the people" are "according to the number of the gods." Both the Lexham English Bible (LEB) and the NASB 2020 updated version provide footnotes to reflect that this verse may be referring to "the angels of God" according to both the LXX[26] and the DSS[27]. There is sufficient evidence to conclude from the LXX, the DSS, ESV, NRSV, LEB and NASB2020 that the people that were scattered at Babel were distributed in such a way that it corresponded with the angels (spiritual beings) that caused their confusion. Regarding the meaning of Deut. 32:8, Craig Keener explains,

> Many scholars prefer the reading of the Septuagint, the pre-Christian translation of the OT, and some Dead Sea Scrolls, which read "according to the sons of God"...This text is closely connected to Ge 10, where 70 nations are listed, but Israel is not included among them. It is possible that, according to the Septuagint, God

---

[26] "LXX" is shorthand for the Septuagint, a Greek translation of the Hebrew Old Testament.
[27] "DSS" is shorthand for the Dead Sea Scrolls.

"divided" (Hebrew prd, in both Ge 10 and this verse) the nations among 70 subordinate, created, divine beings.... This reading is increasingly favored by scholars.[28]

If any doubt should still remain, Deut 32:17 explains how the people were later misled to offer sacrifices (an act of worship) to these spiritual beings, which Moses now identifies as "demons" (*shedim*). In Deut 32:17 Moses says that some *elohim* are *shedim*—some (though not all) spiritual beings are demons.

To put it succinctly, when Yahweh said "let Us go down and there confuse their language..." (Gen 11:7 LSB), the "Us" is referring to other spiritual beings. Those confusing spiritual beings scattered with the people when they were dispersed at Babel. As the people spread out, the spirits spread out with them and the people eventually began to offer sacrifices of worship to these spiritual beings. This is why we have so many different people speaking so many different languages living in so many different places worshiping so many different gods.

Arnold succinctly states that the result of the scattering of the people and their being entrusted to the confusing spirits is that they will be influenced (at least)

---

[28] Craig Keener, *The IVP Bible Background Commentary: New Testament*. (Downers Grove, IL: InterVarsity Press, 2013), Note on Dt 32:8.

or ruled (at worst) by the spirits; "This verse [Deut 32:8] strongly affirms God's sovereignty over all people and nations but also informs us that He has given angels a measure of responsibility over the nations of the earth."[29] Arnold Goes on to say: "This passage is best explained as teaching that 'all nations of the earth are given over into the control of angelic powers.'[30] Finally, Arnold concludes: "The same chapter that reveals the allotments of humanity to angelic guardianship (Dt. 32.8) speaks of Israel provoking God to jealousy by embracing foreign gods (Dt. 32.16). In reality, however, 'they sacrificed to demons.'"[31]

If you're still following along at this point, what we've established here is that Moses understood the scattering of the people at Babel to be a meaningful event. The people that scattered were distributed in such a way that it corresponded to the confusing spirits that scattered them. Further, the people began to make offerings to those confusing spirits.

Israel, since it was not a people at this point, became an exception. Yahweh Himself makes a covenant with Abram in Gen 12 to be his God. Israel is not ruled by confusing spirits or demons, but by Yahweh. This idea is further developed in Dan 10:21 when the

---

[29] Clinton Arnold, *Three Crucial Questions about Spiritual Warfare*. (Grand Rapids, MI: Baker Academic, 1997), 150.
[30] Arnold, *Powers of Darkness*, 63.
[31] Arnold, *Three Questions*, 152.

(arch)angel Michael is identified as Daniel's (and presumably all of Israel's) prince-angel, whereas nations like Persia and Greece have angelic princes that resist the will of Yahweh.

The Captivity and Second Temple Period

Nearly 1,000 years pass between the Song of Moses in Deut 32 and the life of Daniel in captivity. Israel has wandered in the wilderness, entered the Promised Land, established Judges and later Kings, divided into two Kingdoms, repeatedly rebelled against God, and had been judged into exile. During these periods Israel compromised and flirted with the gods of the gentile nations. Each flirtation results in a confrontation with Yahweh, often mediated through prophets.

A fascinating account takes place in Daniel 10. In the midst of a fast Daniel receives a visitation from a spiritual figure that is so intense that Daniel passes out (Dan 10:9). Upon waking up Daniel is comforted by a messenger. It is not completely clear who this spiritual figure is, some suggest the pre-incarnate Christ, others an angelic messenger. In any event, the spiritual figure relays how He has come to Daniel in response to his words (prayers of intercession). This spiritual figure was opposed for twenty-one days by another being called the "prince of Persia" (Dan 10:13). The prince of Persia was only overcome when the angel Michael, described as a "chief prince" (Dan 10:13) provided assistance. Furthermore, this spiritual figure anticipated another fight with the prince of Persia and to also encounter the prince of Greece.

The spiritual nature of this experience, along with the fact that Michael himself is called a "prince" indicates that the princes of Persia and Greece are not human rulers, but spiritual ones—and wicked ones at that. Based on this passage it appears that there are specific spirits arranged in some sort of hierarchy, exercising some sort of authority over the nations of Persia and Greece (and presumably other nations as well). These two spirits, in particular, seemed opposed to the will of Yahweh. Arnold comments on this passage:

> While the book of Daniel does not describe precisely how the angels exert their control over nations, later Jewish tradition is more explicit. The ruling angels over nations, other than Israel, function as deceiving angels. One Jewish text teaches; '[there are] many nations and many people, and they all belong to him [God], but over all of them he caused spirits to rule so that they might lead them astray from following him' (Jubilees 15:31).[32]

---

[32] Arnold, *Powers of Darkness*, 64.

The Second Temple period that followed shortly after Daniel produced a view of evil spirits that identified both specialization and organization among evil spirits. While potentially going beyond what can be clearly affirmed in the Old Testament, the literature of the Second Temple period sheds some light on the worldview of the New Testament:

> This literature is extremely important as we approach the New Testament since it gives us a glimpse into the Judaism of Jesus' day and the time of Paul's ministry. It helps us see the teaching of Jesus and Paul on Satan's kingdom with a new freshness and vitality. Jewish demonology is also important for us because of the significant formative influence it had on the development of early-Christian angelology and demonology as seen by many of the church fathers.[33]

Mullen confirms what Arnold suggests:

> Despite the general tendency for the members of the council to remain in the background, the development of some specialized functions and figures, such as those of Satan, are apparent, especially toward the intertestamental period. The collection of the divine beings constituting

---

[33] Arnold, *Powers of Darkness*, 65.

> the assembly provided a basis for the development of an elaborate angelology wherein there were specific ranks of divine beings. (Dan. 8:16; 9:21; 10:13,21; Tob. 12:15; 1 Enoch 81:5; 87:2-3; 88:1; 90:21-22; 2 Esdras 5:20, etc.)[34]

The Hebrew concept of the Divine Council evolves throughout the Old Testament as well as the Second Temple period. By the time the New Testament is being written Israel has developed a more comprehensive view of angels, demons, powers, principalities, rulers, and authorities. Heiser, seeing a connection between the Old Testament Divine Council and New Testament powers and principalities comments:

> The idea that corrupt gods (sons of God) both populate and control certain geographical regions was still prevalent in the New Testament era. Paul could be referring to geographical terminology and spiritual entities when he refers to principalities, rulers, thrones, authorities, powers and dominions (e.g. Eph 6:12).[35]

Now that the connection between the Hebrew concept of the Divine Council and the New Testament concept of

---

[34] Mullen, *Divine Council*, 14.
[35] Michael Heiser, "Deuteronomy 32:8-9 and the Old Testament Worldview" in *Faithlife Study Bible*. (Grand Rapids, MI: Zondervan, 2017).

powers and principalities has been established, it's time to see how the apostles approached this topic.

Chapter 3:
The New Testament Concept of Powers and Principalities

Nearly half a millennia passes between the final Old Testament reference to the Divine Council and the writing of the New Testament. While the concept of an elaborate and complex spiritual world is carried over from the Old Testament to the New Testament, the terminology shifts somewhat to reflect differences in language, culture, and worldview. For instance, while present in the Old Testament, the use of terms like "angel" and "demon" explodes in the New Testament, relative to the sizes of the testaments. Furthermore, a semi-hierarchical conception of evil spirits emerges that is referred to as "powers, principalities, rulers, and authorities" among other terms.

Paul did not create these terms out of thin air. In fact, "Most scholars believe Paul's vocabulary for the powers reflects the Jewish demonology of his own day. All of the terms Paul used for the powers can be found in Jewish documents of the Greco-Roman period."[36] Keener gives a thorough explanation:

> Paul uses standard terms of his day for the demonic and angelic powers of work behind the political structures of the world, powers that were

---
[36] Arnold, *Powers of Darkness*, 90.

thought to direct earthly rulers and peoples. Jewish people commonly believed that the heavenly powers ruled all the nations except Israel…Jewish people especially viewed these heavenly powers as 'angels of the nations,' spiritual beings who stood behind earthly rulers and guided their rule…Such beings were the ultimate expression of the spiritual division among different peoples, but Paul says that this distinction has been transcended in Christ…[37]

Since these terms were common to Paul and are not uncommon in the New Testament it is beneficial to define them. The *Evangelical Dictionary of Theology* defines principalities and powers as:

> … intermediate beings lower than God and higher than man…principalities (archai) and authorities (exousia) or powers (dynameis) refer to cosmic intelligences, occasionally angelic but usually demonic…other similar spirit powers are dominions (kyriotetes), thrones (thronoi), and rulers (archontes) of this age.[38]

This definition explains these beings as "lower than God." This reflects the importance of the distinction between the terms *elohim* and Yahweh explained

---

[37] Keener, *Background Commentary*, 543.
[38] Elwell, *Evangelical Dictionary*, 956.

previously, as these beings referred to as "lower than God" were actually called "gods" in the Old Testament. What the Evangelical Dictionary of Theology is saying is that these intermediate beings are lower than Yahweh, the one true creator-God who solely possesses non-communicable attributes like omniscience, omnipotence, and omnipresence.

Further, Keener provides this definition; "'Authorities and powers' were angelic rulers over the nations, of which Jewish texts often speak."[39] Keener acknowledges the presence of these terms in 2nd Temple and inter-testamental texts. He also identifies them as angels and rulers who had influence over nations. Further still, "[John Stott and P.T. O'Brien] insist, first, that the principalities and powers must be supernatural beings, since they are confronted by Christ 'in the heavenly places' (Eph. 1:20; 3:10; 6:12)."[40] Finally, the *Jewish Annotated New Testament* describes these beings as "Earthly and demonic forces."[41]

In short, the powers, principalities, rulers, and authorities of the New Testament are rebellious spiritual beings who mislead nations, negatively influence society, and deceive people. For the purposes of this work,

---

[39] Keener, *Background Commentary*, 718.
[40] Elwell, *Evangelical Dictionary*, 956.
[41] Shira L. Lander, "The First Letter of Paul to the Corinthians," in *The Jewish Annotated New Testament*, ed. Amy-Jill Levine and Marc Zvi Brettler, 2nd ed. (New York: Oxford University Press, 2017), 349.

"powers, principalities, rulers, and authorities" will be abbreviated as "powers and principalities" and where necessary appropriate distinctions will be made.

It is important to note that the nature of the powers and principalities can be understood by considering their limited attributes. For instance, since only Yahweh is all-present, these lesser spiritual beings must not be all present. Since they cannot be everywhere at once (unlike Yahweh), they must be limited in time and space. While Yahweh is universal, the powers and principalities must be local. They can only be at one place at one time. In fact, it seems implied by the Babel narrative that they in fact have the ability to travel and scatter abroad, at least to some degree. Whether their ability to scatter is dependent upon a human host is unclear.

Further, since Yahweh is the only spiritual being that is all-knowing, these spiritual beings are limited in their knowledge. It is not clear what the intellectual capacities of powers and principalities are, but it should be assumed that they can remember, learn and think. While powers and principalities are not eternal like Yahweh, they appear to have been present at creation (Job 38:7) and have been compiling data and experiences for millennia. Referring to the "manifold wisdom of God" (Eph 3:10 NASB) being made known to the powers and principalities, the *Evangelical Dictionary of Theology* lists the ability to learn as one of the "Six acts in the drama of the principalities and powers"[42] Suffice it to say, powers and principalities have had a significant amount of time to observe how the universe operates and what methods of manipulation humans are susceptible to. Their strategies have been tested and refined over time.

Finally, since only Yahweh is all-powerful, powers and principalities are not. These lesser spirits seem limited in their abilities. This may provide some insight into why ancient pantheons would assign certain tasks to specific deities. Whether evil spirits are specialists is not clear, but certainly, there are different types of evil spirits and they do not all manifest in the same way or to the same degree in the New Testament.

Powers and Principalities in 1 Peter, Romans, and 1 Corinthians

Most of the New Testament data related to powers and principalities comes from the Apostle Paul. However, the Apostle Peter does make one reference in his first epistle. The fact that Peter references this concept establishes that this was not a uniquely Pauline idea but was likely common among first century Jews.

In 1 Peter 3:18-22, Peter makes a curious and confusing statement about Jesus preaching to imprisoned spirits. These imprisoned spirits are described as

---

[42] Elwell, *Evangelical Dictionary*, 956.

"disobedient" during the "days of Noah" (1 Pe 3:20 NASB). Perhaps this is a reference to the rebellious sons of God that are related to the Nephilim in Genesis 6. It was their rebellion that provoked (at least in part) the flood of Noah's day.

Peter explains how the ark corresponds to baptism and also that Jesus is presently at the right hand of God in heaven, having subjected "angels, authorities and powers" to Himself (1 Pe 3:22 NASB). While Peter does not explicitly state the nature of the correlation between the rebellious sons of God of Genesis 6 and the powers and principalities of the New Testament, he does establish some correlation.

The thrust of the passage however seems to be that Jesus established dominance in the spiritual realm by subjecting "angels, authorities, and powers." Aside from one reference in the epistles of Peter, most of the remaining New Testament data regarding powers and principalities is provided by Paul.

In Romans 8:31-39 Paul asks a series of rhetorical questions, the purpose of which appears to be to assure the Roman Christians of their salvation. The rhetorical questions in vs. 31-34 would lead the readers to believe that no opposition against them will overtake God's favor for them, that the same God who sacrificially provided His own Son would not then become withholding and stingy toward other needs, and that no condemnatory charge against them would stand in God's judgment.

Paul spends significant time developing the rhetorical question is vs. 35 - in fact, he essentially answers the question himself. The question is; "Who will separate us from the love of Christ?" He posits some common objections that he might anticipate, i.e. tribulation, distress, persecution, etc. but assures the readers that none of these challenging consequences would successfully separate them from God's love for His redeemed people.

Building his argument, Paul then provides a list of additional items that are unable to separate the Roman Christians from God's love in vs. 38. For the most part, the list is a series of antithetical ideas. For instance, Paul writes that "neither death, nor life" or "things present, nor things to come" or "height, nor depth" will be able to separate them from God's love. Tucked into the list of antithetical items is "nor angels, nor principalities." The antithetical nature of angels and principalities in this passage suggests strongly that angels are good and principalities are evil. "Given the context of cosmic opposition here, we should take 'principalities' and 'powers' (KJV, NASB) with 'angels' as referring to the spiritual forces ruling the nations and bringing opposition against God's people."[43] In this comment from Keener we further establish the connection between

---

[43] Keener, *Background Commentary*, 432.

the Divine Council (at least the rebellious elements) and powers and principalities.

The idea that powers and principalities are evil (spirits) is further developed in 1 Cor 15:20-26. In this passage, Paul is explaining the power of Christ's resurrection and the implications of that power at Christ's return. According to Paul, Jesus has "abolished" or destroyed "all rule (ἀρχή), and all authority (ἐξουσία) and power (δύναμις)." The *Dictionary of Demons and Deities in the Bible* explains; "...it is clear that the ἀρχή, along with every authority and power, are considered hostile, since they are subject to destruction and are parallel to the term 'enemies' in 1 Cor. 15:25...."[44]

Powers and Principalities in Ephesians

Paul's epistles to the church in Ephesus provide a unique and insightful look into his understanding of powers and principalities. Ephesians, unlike Paul's other epistles, is not written to address a specific error in the church. Instead, Ephesians is Paul's opportunity to build a comprehensive New Testament theology of the spiritual world. This might indicate that Ephesians was intended to be a circular letter that would be distributed to as many churches as possible regardless of context or circumstances. *The Jewish Annotated New Testament* elaborates,

---

[44] Van Der Toorn, *Deities and Demons*, 79.

The form of the letter is quite unlike Paul's occasional letter, written in response to particular historical circumstances and delivered to a given audience. It has been characterized as a circular letter, one that, by design, speaks not to a single community but to various audiences to which it might be circulated.[45]

Paul's use of phrases like 'heavenly places" (Eph 1:3, 1:20, 2:6, 3:10, and 6:12) reveals that Paul has spiritual concepts in mind. Further, Paul informs the Ephesians about the spiritual transformations and transactions that took place upon their conversion; the sealing of the Holy Spirit upon their lives (Eph 1:13 and 4:30) as well as the new identity that they have inherited. Paul explains that they are now "seated with Christ in heavenly places" (Eph 2:6) and that they are to be "strengthened with power through His Spirit in the inner man" (Eph 3:16). The entire epistle is replete with spiritual realities.

One of those spiritual realities is the current state of powers and principalities in light of Christ's death and resurrection. In the midst of an apostolic prayer in Ephesians 1, Paul reminds his readers that Christ is

---

[45] David Kraemer, "The Letter of Paul to the Ephesians," in *The Jewish Annotated New Testament*, ed. Amy-Jill Levine and Marc Zvi Brettler, 2nd ed. (New York: Oxford University Press, 2017), 388.

presently seated in heavenly places, "far above all rule and authority and power and dominion, and every name that is named." (Eph 1:21) As in 1 Cor 15; "There can be little doubt that the powers mentioned in Eph 1:21 and 6:12, and specifically the *archai* must be understood as evil supernatural powers."[46] Further, Eph 2:2, likely referring to Satan or the Devil speaks of "the ruler of the power of the air, the spirit that is now at work among those who are disobedient." Jesus is said to be seated "far above" these evil supernatural powers as a result of His death, resurrection, and exaltation.

    Later, in Eph 3:8-10 Paul elaborates on another dynamic that's unfolding in the heavenly places. Through Paul's preaching and through the faithfulness of the church; "the manifold [varied, multi-faceted] wisdom of God might now be made known through the church to the rulers and the authorities in the heavenly places." (Eph 3:10 NASB). These evil spiritual beings are learning for themselves how multi-faceted and comprehensive the wisdom of God is. The primary way in which God's wisdom is revealed is in the person of Jesus Christ (Eph 3:8). Jesus Christ appears to be the answer to many cliff-hangers like; "How will God reconcile man to Himself?" and "How will God reclaim authority over the earth for mankind?" and "How will God defeat death?" The answer to all of these questions

---

[46] Van Der Toorn, *Deities and Demons*, 79.

and more are found in Jesus Christ and the powers and principalities are learning these lessons in real time.

For Paul, it was not enough to simply inform the Ephesians of the spiritual realm (something they were no doubt already aware of—perhaps this was more of a reminder) but he called them to engage the spiritual realm, specifically in a spiritual battle. In Ephesians 6:10-20 Paul expects believers in Jesus to "stand firm against the schemes of the devil" (Eph 6:11). In the subsequent verses, Paul elaborates on how this might be done. First, in keeping with the tone of the entire epistle, he reminds his readers that the battle is spiritual, not natural; "our struggle is not against flesh and blood...." (Eph 6:12). The implications of this statement are wide-ranging. At the very least Paul is saying that the battle is not against physical enemies. He could also very well be saying that the battle is neither political, social or cultural.

Powers and Principalities in Colossians

Like Ephesians, the epistle to the Colossians is heavily concerned with spiritual realities. Unlike Ephesians, Paul is addressing some false teachings that have made their way into the church in Colossae, often referred to as the "Colossian heresy". The Colossian heresy is difficult to fully reconstruct from the text of the epistle, but it clearly had elements of mysticism that resulted in the worship of angels (perhaps an allusion to

Deut 32:17) and confident assertions about spiritual visions (Col 2:18). The *Jewish Annotated New Testament* summarizes this error; "The theologians of this young church have placed the Christ ("the Anointed One") on the same level as angels (2:18), the 'elemental spirits of the universe' (2:8), and 'rulers and authorities' (2:15)..."[47] To put Christ and angels on the same level is either to demote Christ or to exalt angels to a place that they do not rightfully hold.

In Colossians 1:13-16 Paul introduces the idea that a transfer took place when the Colossian Christians put their faith in Christ. Paul describes the nature of this transfer as moving "from the domain of darkness" and to "the Kingdom of His beloved son" (Col 1:13 NASB). Clearly, there is a change of allegiance and even ownership when this transfer takes place. The Colossians Christians are now members of a totally new Kingdom and follow a new ruler—a spiritual ruler.

In verse 15 Paul refers to Jesus as the "firstborn of all creation." Since Paul and other New Testament writers make it clear elsewhere that Jesus was not a created being (Jn 1, Heb 1, etc), this verse should not be understood as saying that Jesus was chronologically the first created being, but rather that Jesus maintains the authority of a firstborn son that was common in that

---

[47] Peter Zaas, "The Letter of Paul to the Colossians," in *The Jewish Annotated New Testament*, ed. Amy-Jill Levine and Marc Zvi Brettler, 2nd ed. (New York: Oxford University Press, 2017), 407.

culture—the authority to oversee and rule. Verse 15 is not referring to the chronological order of creation, but the hierarchical order of creation.

In verse 16 Paul states unequivocally that Jesus created all things—both heavenly and earthly things. Among those things that Jesus created are "thrones or dominions or rulers or authorities." This seems to indicate that Jesus created the demonic powers that animate the evil in society and social systems. Clearly, these powers are in rebellion against Jesus, as they do not reflect the nature and character of Jesus revealed throughout the New Testament. Essentially, these thrones, dominions, rulers, and authorities do not rule in the same manner that Jesus rules. This harkens back to the rebuke of the *elohim* in Ps 82.

Just a few verses later, Col 2:10 explains that Jesus is the head over all "rule and authority". Paul is saying that even while these evil powers are in rebellion, Jesus still maintains authority over them—that even in their rebellion they are subject to Him and that He has not lost or surrendered His sovereignty.

Colossians 2:15 explains how Jesus has already triumphed over and defeated the rulers and authorities. Jesus defeated these evil spirits at the cross (Col 2:14-15). Not only did He defeat them, but they were also disarmed and publicly ridiculed. As the *Jewish Annotated New Testament* points out, for the evil spirits to be disarmed and ridiculed is essentially for them to be left naked and humiliated.[48]

The cross of Jesus was the definitive, historical act that resulted in the defeat of the rebellious spirits and the triumph of Jesus, as Arnold observes: "Although He was always sovereign because He was the Creator, Christ still needed to defeat those rebellious powers. The cross, resurrection, and exaltation of Christ are the basis for His victory over the powers."[49]

The language of verse 15 invokes a common image at the time, that of a victorious king parading his vanquished foes through the streets, making a "public display of them." While many would view the cross as a defeat for Jesus and a victory for evil, Paul viewed the cross (and the subsequent resurrection and exaltation of Jesus) as a victory for Jesus and a defeat for the evil powers.

The fact that Jesus both created and defeated these evil spiritual beings should be sufficient to convince the Colossians that Jesus alone, not angels, is worthy of their worship.

---

[48] Zaas, "Colossians," 413.
[49] Arnold, *Powers of Darkness*, 109.

Chapter 4:
Why This Matters (Pt. 2)

The relationship between the Divine Council and powers and principalities has real-life implications for those who read, believe, and follow the Bible. As followers of Jesus must adopt a spiritual or supernatural worldview that acknowledges a singular creator-God who alone has attributes like omnipresence, omnipotence, and omniscience, while also allowing for other lesser spiritual beings who may have limited abilities. This essentially demands the acknowledgment of the existence of angels and demons at the very least.

Further, it becomes clear that only Christ/Yahweh is worthy of worship and that worship directed toward lesser spiritual beings was considered by both Moses (Deut 32:17) and Paul (1 Cor 10:20) as demonic and unacceptable.

Additionally, the same confusing spirits that misled and scattered the nations at Babel are disarmed by Jesus at the Cross. As a result, Jesus sends His people on a mission to obtain representatives from every family, nation, and language, unifying them in Christ/Yahweh, resulting in all nations and tongues offering praise to the one true God (Mt 24:14; 28:18-20, Rev 7:9).

As the church advances the mission and reign of Christ, it should recognize that various geographical, cultural, social, and political dynamics may at times be the result of the influence of evil spirits and will thus need to confront those dynamics accordingly. For instance, churches in a region may need to join forces when confronting a regional power or principality.

Finally, the nature of the conflict between the church and powers and principalities must be clear. While the battle may manifest itself in cultural, social, or political realities, it is primarily a spiritual conflict (Eph 6:12) between spiritual entities. One spiritual entity is described as "naked" and "humiliated"[50] while the other is clothed in the full armor of God, fully equipped with a shield and sword (Eph 6:11-17).

The battle that was initiated in the Garden of Eden in Gen 3 was accelerated at the Tower of Babel in Gen 11. At the cross, Jesus defeated the spirits that scattered the people at Babel and the church is currently engaged in the worldwide work of redeeming a representative from every language and ethnicity to the right worship of the true God, Yahweh the God of Abraham. Upon the completion of His mission, Jesus will have worshipers from each people group that had previously been influenced or ruled by rebellious Divine Council members known as "powers and principalities."

---

[50] Zaas, "Colossians," 413.

BIBLIOGRAPHY

Arnold, Clinton E. *Powers of Darkness: Principalities and Powers in Paul's Letters.* Downers Grove, IL: IVP Academic, 1992.

_____. *Three Crucial Questions about Spiritual Warfare.* Grand Rapids, MI: Baker Academic, 1997

Bible Project, "Elohim," Feb. 28th, 2019, https://youtu.be/U5iyUik97Lg

Briggs, Charles A., Francis Brown and S.R. Driver, *The Brown-Driver-Briggs Hebrew and English Lexicon.* Peabody, MA: Hendrickson Publications, 1996

Carson, D. A. ed. *NIV Biblical Theology Study Bible,* Grand Rapids, MI: Zondervan, 2018.

Elwell, Walter A. ed, *Evangelical Dictionary of Theology, 2nd Ed.* Grand Rapids, MI: Baker Academic, 2006

Heiser, Michael S. "Divine Council" in *Dictionary of the Old Testament: Wisdom, Poetry and Writings* edited by Peter Enns and Tremper

Longman III, 112-116. Downers Grove, IL: IVP Academic, 2008.

_____. "Divine Council" in *Dictionary of Old Testament: Prophets* edited by Mark J. Boda and J. Gordon McConville, 162-166. Downers Grove, IL: IVP Academic, 2012.

_____. *The Unseen Realm: Recovering the Supernatural Worldview of the Bible.* Bellingham, WA: Lexham Press, 2015

_____. "Deuteronomy 32:8-9 and the Old Testament Worldview" in *Faithlife Study Bible*. Grand Rapids, MI: Zondervan, 2017.

Keener, Craig. *The IVP Bible Background Commentary: New Testament.* Downers Grove, IL: InterVarsity Press, 2013.

_____. and Walton, John, *"Divine Council" article in the NIV Cultural Backgrounds Study Bible.* Grand Rapids, MI: Zondervan, 2016

Kraemer, David. "The Letter of Paul to the Ephesians." Pages 388–97 in *The Jewish Annotated New Testament*. Edited by Amy-Jill Levine and Marc Zvi Brettler. 2nd ed. New York: Oxford University Press, 2017.

Lander, Shira L. "The First Letter of Paul to the Corinthians." Pages 321–51 in *The Jewish Annotated*

New Testament. Edited by Amy-Jill Levine and Marc Zvi Brettler. 2nd ed. New York: Oxford University Press, 2017.

Levine, Amy-Jill and Brettler, Marc Zvi eds. *The Jewish Annotated New Testament: Second Edition.* New York, NY: Oxford University Press, 2011

Meier, Samuel A. *Themes and Transformations in Old Testament Prophecy*. Downers Grove, IL: IVP Academic, 2009.

Mullen Jr., E. T. *The Divine Council in Canaanite and Early Hebrew Literature.* Ann Arbor, MI: Brill Publishing, 1980.

_____. "Divine Assembly" in *The Anchor Yale Bible Dictionary* edited by David Noel Freedman. New York: Doubleday, 1992.

Pew Research Center, "10 facts about atheists," Dec. 6th, 2019, https://www.pewresearch.org/fact-tank/2019/12/06/10-facts-about-atheists/

Van Der Toorn, Karl, Bob Becking and Pieter W. Van Der Horst, eds. *Dictionary of Deities and Demons in the Bible*. Leiden, The Netherlands: Brill Publishing, 1999.

Walton, John H., *Ancient Near Eastern Thought and the Old Testament 2nd Ed.* Grand Rapids, MI: Baker Academic, 2018.

Zaas, Peter. "The Letter of Paul to the Colossians." Pages 407–18 in *The Jewish Annotated New Testament*. Edited by Amy-Jill Levine and Marc Zvi Brettler. 2nd ed. New York: Oxford University Press, 2017.

Made in the USA
Middletown, DE
08 June 2022

Many Christians are aware of the obstacles and opportunities associated with the rise in atheism and agnosticism over the past 20 years. But even with the rise in atheism and agnosticism, the vast majority of the world (over 90%) still believe in some sort of god or higher power.

In this brief work, James Rudd presents a Biblical perspective on world religions, religious pluralism, polytheism, spiritual warfare and territorial spirits. He attempts to answer the question; "Why do we have so many different people, speaking so many different languages, living in so many different places, worshiping so many different gods—and what does that mean for followers of Jesus?"

This brief explanation traces the Hebrew concept of the Divine Council throughout the Old Testament and into the New Testament, where the concept began to be referred to as "powers and principalities" and what is now commonly referred to as "territorial spirits." This work is somewhat technical, but can be read in under an hour.

Rev. James Rudd has been a pastor since 2004. He has a B.S. in Bible and Pastoral Ministry from Nyack College and an M.A. in Biblical Studies from Alliance Theological Seminary. He is also ordained with the Christian and Missionary Alliance. Currently, he lives in Philadelphia with his wife and three children. You can connect with him at reverencejournal.com.

ISBN 9798821386618